The Campus History Series

IOWA WESLEYAN UNIVERSITY

This aerial photograph of the Iowa Wesleyan campus in Mount Pleasant, Iowa, can be dated by examining the buildings. The German College at bottom center was removed in 1961. Sheaffer-Trieschmann Hall, visible at top center, was built in 1953. There is no Holland Student Union, which was constructed in 1957. Thus, the image dates from 1953 to 1956. (Courtesy of Iowa Wesleyan's archives.)

ON THE FRONT COVER: Long skirts and capri pants were hallmarks of 1950s fashion. These students are entering the new Sheaffer-Trieschmann Hall, which had replaced Hershey Hall as the female dormitory in 1953. (Courtesy of Iowa Wesleyan's archives.)

COVER BACKGROUND: Female students sit outside Hershey Hall in 1920. The 1925–1926 Hershey Hall house regulations noted, "Should it be necessary to leave the Hall after 10:00 p.m. or to leave or enter the Hall before 7:00 a.m., arrangements should be made in advance with the Hall Superintendent." (Courtesy of Iowa Wesleyan's archives.)

The Campus History Series

IOWA WESLEYAN UNIVERSITY

JEFFREY MEYER

ARCADIA
PUBLISHING

Published by Arcadia Publishing
Charleston, South Carolina

Printed in the United States of America

Library of Congress Control Number: 2022946572

For all general information, please contact Arcadia Publishing:
Telephone 843-853-2070
Fax 843-853-0044
E-mail sales@arcadiapublishing.com
For customer service and orders:
Toll-Free 1-888-313-2665

Visit us on the Internet at www.arcadiapublishing.com

*This book is dedicated to Joy and Ed Conwell,
whose years of work in the university archives
preserved the memory of this institution.*

CONTENTS

ACKNOWLEDGMENTS

This book is the result of careful curation of Iowa Wesleyan's archives. Joy Conwell was a critical component of the university community for 20 years until her passing in 2021. Under her curation, the university archives were well managed, organized, and preserved. The university is forever indebted to her commitment to the institution's history, and generations to come will have the resources to research and appreciate the students, staff, and faculty who went before. Her invisible hand is present here. All images in this work are derived from Iowa Wesleyan's archives except for an image created by NASA.

The author thanks Provost DeWayne Frazier for the opportunity to write this book. The author would also like to thank Esther Wonderlich, the Methodist archivist who works in the Chadwick Library, for her graciousness during the regular interruptions into her workspace while research for the book was being conducted. Caitrin Cunningham of Arcadia Publishing was very helpful throughout the publishing process. Kendra Hefner provided some images from recent years. Finally, Michelle, the author's wife, is very patient in listening to ideas of various degrees of general interest.

INTRODUCTION

The foundations of Iowa Wesleyan University were set in place less than 10 years after the first pioneers arrived in the area, contributing to Mount Pleasant's early designation as "the Athens of Iowa." Presley Saunders established the first pioneer lodging along a spring in present Saunders Park in 1834. In 1835, when Mount Pleasant was but a collection of frontier cabins, Methodist circuit rider Rev. John Ruble preached among the pioneers. Mount Pleasant officially became the social, political, and legal center of the county in 1839 with the building of the first courthouse in the town square.

The spirit of Methodism followed the first pioneers to Mount Pleasant. Methodism brought several progressive ideas to the Iowa frontier. Education, abolition, and female enfranchisement were primary features of early Iowan philosophy. The Iowa Annual Conference of the Methodist Episcopal Church in 1854 consisted of committees for the causes of abolition and temperance, as well as the procurement of funds for education. The 1854 conference reported 422 Methodist members in Mount Pleasant, the largest Methodist community in the Burlington District and one of the largest in the state.

The flowering of Methodism in early Mount Pleasant, the town's designation as a county seat, and the Iowa Territory's progressive views on education made fertile soil for the planting of a college. In 1840, the Territorial Legislature of Iowa passed "an Act to establish a university at the town of Mt. Pleasant, in Henry county [*sic*]." The movement to create a university developed further in 1842 following "an act to incorporate the Mount Pleasant Literary Institute." The act stipulated that E. Kilpatrick, Samuel Brazelton, and others "are hereby ordained, constituted and declared, a body corporate, by the name of 'The Mount Pleasant Literary Institute.' " The act of 1842 included a stipulation declaring: "No religious test of admission. That said institution shall be under charge of the Methodist Episcopal Church, but there shall be no religious test for the admission of students to said institute." The legislature approved this act on February 17, 1842. Iowa Wesleyan's birth and the official birth of Mount Pleasant as an incorporated city were in the same year, 1842.

The community provided for the new academic institution. Local landowners donated the grounds for the school. Rev. Aristides Huestis raised money for the first building, later known as Pioneer Hall. In use by 1846, Pioneer Hall is among the oldest academic buildings still in use west of the Mississippi River. This two-story building featured classroom space, laboratory equipment, a library collection, and even housing for the university president.

The university's second decade, the 1850s, was a critical moment for the new institute, the town of Mount Pleasant, and the United States. Iowa Wesleyan's early years coincided with the intense sectional differences dividing the country. The Compromise of 1850, which allowed California to enter the Union as a free state, also saw the passage of the Fugitive Slave Act, which required citizens living in free states like Iowa to return escaped slaves to their owners in slave states. The proximity of Missouri to Iowa made these issues particularly intense. The Kansas-Nebraska Act of 1854—which made it a possibility that Kansas or Nebraska could enter the Union as slave states—invigorated Iowa's abolitionists.

This historical context is needed to understand Iowa Wesleyan's president at that time, James Harlan, and how he became a critical figure. President Harlan, an abolitionist and scholar, advocated for the establishment of a second and much larger academic building on campus. In 1855, his efforts became a reality. The building, Old Main, provided the necessary space to establish a proper academic institution, including more classrooms, a larger library room, a museum, and scientific laboratories. Also in 1855, President Harlan received a new vocation following his election to the US Senate. Harlan brought Iowa's progressive tone to Washington, DC, where he befriended President Lincoln. Senator Harlan's signature is on the Thirteenth Amendment, the document that abolished slavery. Thus, Iowa Wesleyan and Mount Pleasant are connected at the national level to the abolition of slavery.

Iowa Wesleyan made further contributions to American progress. While Senator Harlan was in Washington, Iowa Wesleyan graduated its first female student, Lucy W. Killpatrick Byrkit, in 1859, long before many institutions even admitted women. Ten years later in 1869, Arabella Babb Mansfield (class of 1866) passed the bar exam, becoming the first female attorney in the United States. It is no stretch of the imagination to see that this institution also produced the first female commander of the International Space Station, Peggy Whitson (1981).

In 1873, the German College was established at Iowa Wesleyan, and a third academic building was built on campus to house it. The German College was also affiliated with Methodism, and courses were taught in German. Iowa Wesleyan, a small academic community, has had an international and multicultural heritage since its beginning.

In the years of the Great Depression, Iowa Wesleyan made important scientific contributions. Prof. Thomas Poulter (1923) participated in an Antarctic expedition with the explorer Rear Adm. Richard Byrd in 1933. In that same decade, physics student James Van Allen (1935) would go on to discover the radiation belts around the Earth, and perform important rocket experiments through the 20th century. Thus, Iowa Wesleyan's 20th-century alumni include a polar explorer, a rocket scientist, and an astronaut.

Other decades left major legacies on the campus as well. The 1890s, under the leadership of President Stafford, saw the addition of the Chapel and Hershey Hall. The 1920s resulted in the construction of the P.E.O. Memorial Library and the Gymnasium. The 1950s added Sheaffer-Trieschmann Hall and the John Wesley Holland Student Union. And the 1960s resulted in the construction of the Trieschmann Hall of Science, McKibbin Hall, and the J. Raymond Chadwick Library.

One

THE PIONEER AGE
1842–1889

Iowa Wesleyan was founded as the Mount Pleasant Literary Institute during the first generation of pioneers in Iowa in 1842, four years before Iowa achieved statehood. The first courses reflected the curriculum of other academies in the mid-19th century. Professors taught courses in classical languages like Greek and Latin—considered necessary for clergy—along with mathematics and the natural sciences. The new institute fell into financial hardship by 1850. After a series of presidential resignations in a short period, the school attempted to rescue itself by recruiting James Harlan, an attorney with school administrative experience in Iowa City.

Harlan was convinced the institute needed a thorough reworking. The school required a much larger building to support more students and a wider college course of study. In the spring of 1853, the trustees followed through with Harlan's vision, embracing a finance campaign of $15,000 for a new building. The first cornerstone was laid on July 4, 1854. The Iowa Conference of the Methodist Episcopal Church noted in 1855 that there were 254 students at the school.

University president James Harlan was elected to the US Senate in 1855. But in his short tenure at the school, Harlan's vision transformed the ailing institution into Iowa Wesleyan University. Ten years later, Senator Harlan—a stalwart Lincoln Republican—signed the Thirteenth Amendment, banishing slavery in the United States, fulfilling Lincoln's legacy after his assassination. Harlan returned to Mount Pleasant following his senatorial career, and his daughter Mary joined the Lincoln family with her marriage to Robert Todd Lincoln.

Iowa Wesleyan was a critical reason why Mount Pleasant earned the title "the Athens of Iowa." In this environment, the students competed not in athletics but in literary societies. The Philomathean Literary Society, founded in 1858, and the Hamline Literary Society, founded in 1855 at President Harlan's suggestion, provided debate competitions for male students. The Ruthean Literary Society, established on campus in 1856, provided a platform for female students. The P.E.O. Sisterhood was founded in Old Main in 1869, providing even more opportunities for women. The establishment of the German College in 1873 began Iowa Wesleyan's long tradition as a multicultural, international academic environment.

Iowa Wesleyan made significant contributions during its pioneer age, graduating its first female student in 1859, Lucy Killpatrick Byrkit. The first female attorney in the nation, Arabella Babb Mansfield, graduated in 1866, and the first African American woman to graduate college in the state of Iowa, Susan Mosely Grandison, graduated from Iowa Wesleyan in 1885.

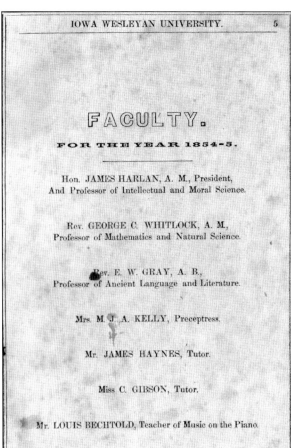

FACULTY.

FOR THE YEAR 1854-5.

Hon. JAMES HARLAN, A. M., President,
And Professor of Intellectual and Moral Science.

Rev. GEORGE C. WHITLOCK, A. M,
Professor of Mathematics and Natural Science.

Rev. E. W. GRAY, A. B.,
Professor of Ancient Language and Literature.

Mrs. M. J. A. KELLY, Preceptress.

Mr. JAMES HAYNES, Tutor.

Miss C. GIBSON, Tutor.

Mr. LOUIS BECHTOLD, Teacher of Music on the Piano.

The university catalog for the academic year 1854–1855 lists James Harlan as president and professor of intellectual and moral science. Rev. George Whitlock was a professor of mathematics and natural science, and Rev. E.W. Gray was a professor of ancient languages and literature. There were also two women on the faculty: Mrs. M.J.A. Kelly, preceptress, and C. Gibson, a tutor.

This 1854 fundraising stationery illustrates the proposed three-story structure that would be Old Main. The notice states that the building "will be one of the most commodious, beautiful and substantial college edifices in the Western States." The text also states that the Territorial Legislature of Iowa had recently changed the name of the school from Mount Pleasant Literary Institute to Iowa Wesleyan University.

THE IOWA WESLEYAN UNIVERSITY,
MOUNT PLEASANT, HENRY COUNTY, IOWA.

Pres. James Harlan was elected to the US Senate in 1855. Harlan played a critical role in the abolition movement, becoming a key ally of Abraham Lincoln. On one occasion, Harlan gave a speech to the Senate, and the nervous senator received encouragement from Charles Sumner of Massachusetts, one of the most prominent abolitionists in Congress.

Pioneer Hall (left) and Old Main (right) are the two oldest academic buildings on campus, providing the early generations of students with classrooms, museum spaces, scientific laboratories, and even housing for the university president. Pioneer Hall was built in 1845 and Old Main was built in 1855.

Records show that the procurement of a college bell was a priority for the university in the 1850s. In an era before the widespread use of portable time-telling devices, bells served a very functional purpose, alerting everyone on campus of the current time.

Lucy Webster Killpatrick Byrkit was the first female graduate of Iowa Wesleyan, receiving her diploma in 1859. Iowa Wesleyan's philosophy advanced the progressive spirit that pervaded Iowa's early history, with female education and enfranchisement among the central tenets of Iowa's foundation.

This portrait of Lucy W. Killpatrick Byrkit was taken in Muscatine, Iowa. Her 1859 graduation was only three years after the university awarded its first bachelor's degree, which went to Winfield Scott Mayne. Women were in the earliest classes.

EXHIBITION

BY THE

PHILOMATHEAN

LITERARY SOCIETY.

OF THE

Iowa Wesleyan University,

MONDAY EVENING,

JUNE 15, 1868,

– ••• – –

Music by WEBBER's String Band.

The Philomathean Literary Society, or "Philo," was organized at Iowa Wesleyan in 1858. The society engaged in oratorical contests, and this exhibition from June 15, 1868, announces a mid-19th-century version of a competitive sport. *Philomathean* is Greek for "lover of study."

Students pose in their theater costumes in 1873. Before the construction of the Chapel in 1893, student productions took place in local Mount Pleasant venues like the Saunders Opera House near the town square.

In the 1870s, Senator Harlan retired with his wife, Ann Eliza, to a residence at the intersection of Broad and Main Streets on the campus of Iowa Wesleyan. He improved upon the original home at that location, expanding the size of the home known today as the Harlan-Lincoln House. Ann Eliza died in 1884, and James remained active in the university and the Methodist Church until his death in 1899.

Myers

FAIRFIELD,
Iowa

Dr. Alexander Rommel founded the Mount Pleasant Conservatory of Music in 1874, which was incorporated into Iowa Wesleyan in 1877. Dr. Rommel was born in Germany, and brought a classical European musical program to Iowa Wesleyan.

This portrait of Arabella Mansfield from about 1875 was taken at the Dyall photography studio on Main Street in Mount Pleasant. In addition to being the first female attorney in the United States, Mansfield was actively involved in the women's enfranchisement movement. In 1870, she served as an officer for the Iowa Woman's Enfranchisement Convention, which was held in Mount Pleasant.

A portrait of Senator Harlan hangs inside the Harlan-Lincoln House. The senator campaigned tirelessly for Abraham Lincoln in 1860, gaining Lincoln's appreciation. He played an important role in President Lincoln's re-election in 1864.

This page from the *Katalog des Deutsches Collegiums* (*Catalog of the German College*) is from the academic year 1874–1875. It discusses the *Verbindung* (connection) between the German College and Iowa Wesleyan University, noting that German College students could take courses at Iowa Wesleyan, and could also use the university's museums.

Vermischte Nachrichten.

Verbindung des Deutschen Collegiums mit der J. W. U.

Einem Uebereinkommen gemäß, welches zwischen den beiden Anstalten getroffen ist, haben unsere Studenten sowohl freien Unterricht in allen Klassen der Iowa Wesleyan Universität, als auch freien Gebrauch des Museums, soweit derselbe zur Erklärung der Wissenschaften erforderlich ist.

Lage, Gebäude u. s. w.

Das „Deutsche Collegium" ist in Mt. Pleasant, einem Städtchen des Staates Iowa, 28 Meilen westlich von Burlington, an der Burlington und Missouri Eisenbahn gelegen. Die Umgegend ist herrlich, das Klima äußerst gesund und der Boden von außerordentlicher Fruchtbarkeit, so daß, obgleich die vergangene Jahreszeit nicht sehr günstig war, doch 75 Bushel des schönsten Welschkorns in vielen Plätzen eingeerntet wurden. Die Einwohnerzahl von Mt. Pleasant beläuft sich auf ungefähr 6000, welche wegen ihrer Moralität rühmlichst bekannt sind und so eben durch öffentliche Abstimmung den Handel in berauschenden Getränken aus der Stadt verbannt haben. Im nördlichen Theile der Stadt liegt unsere Anstalt, anziehend durch ihr Aeußeres, in einem fünf Acker enthaltenden Areale. Im modernen Style, von Backsteinen einfach aber geschmackvoll erbaut, drei Stockwerke hoch, bildet es mit den ihm gegenüber liegenden Gebäuden der J. W. U., die Hauptzierde dieses Stadttheiles. Das Gebäude enthält Raum genug für mehr Studenten, als wir jetzt haben.

Studien-Cursus.

Dieser umfaßt drei Departements :

1) Den theologischen Cursus, drei Jahre umfassend.
2) Den classischen Cursus, vier Jahre umfassend.
3) Den wissenschaftlichen Cursus, ebenfalls vier Jahre umfassend.

Diesen geht ein Vorbereitungs-Cursus voran, welcher auf zwei Jahre festgesetzt ist.

Literarische Gesellschaft.

Eine solche hat sich unter dem Namen, der „Schiller-Verein," gebildet. Der adoptirten Constitution gemäß, steht sie sowohl jungen Männern als jungen Mädchen offen, und ist es der Zweck derselben, den Schülern des Collegiums noch mehr Gelegenheit zu verschaffen, sich im Gebrauche der deutschen Sprache auszubilden.

Es ist keinem der Studenten des Deutschen Collegiums erlaubt, sich einer der in der J. W. U. bestehenden literarischen Gesellschaften anzuschließen; es sei denn, daß derselbe auch ein Mitglied des Schiller-Vereins ist und sich verpflichtet, dem Letzteren in seinen Leistungen den Vorgang zu geben.

In den Verhandlungen des Schiller-Vereins wird nur die deutsche Sprache gestattet.

Members of the class of 1882 pose with their boulder. On a nice May afternoon in 1882, students went for a picnic at the Skunk River. On the way, they spotted a boulder not to be missed, and hauled it back to campus. It is still on the college green west of Old Main with "Class '82" chiseled on its face.

In 1856, twenty female students formed Iowa Wesleyan's Ruthean Literary Society, just one year after the first male literary society, the Hamline Society. This 1883 card advertises an open house in the "college chapel." Before the construction of the Chapel, the college chapel was a room in Old Main.

This notice from the Oratorical Association publicizes a speaking contest to be held on Tuesday, January 20, 1885. Belle A. Mansfield, the first female lawyer in the nation, is listed as a contest judge. These speaking contests featured discussions of important issues of the day as well as philosophical topics.

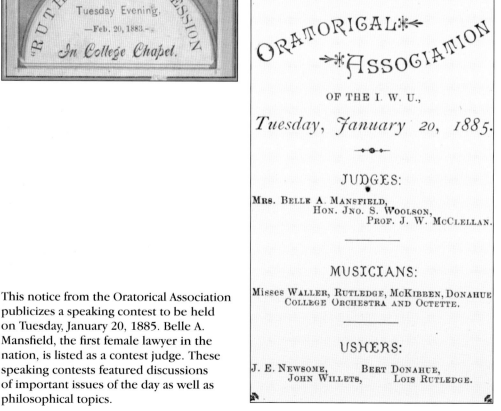

ORATORICAL CONTEST,

Given under the auspices of the

ORATORICAL ASSOCIATION

OF THE I. W. U.,

Tuesday, January 20, 1885.

JUDGES:

Mrs. Belle A. Mansfield,
Hon. Jno. S. Woolson,
Prof. J. W. McClellan.

MUSICIANS:

Misses Waller, Rutledge, McKibben, Donahue
College Orchestra and Octette.

USHERS:

J. E. Newsome,   Bert Donahue,
   John Willets,   Lois Rutledge.

Susan Mosely Grandison was the first African American to graduate from Iowa Wesleyan. Born in Missouri in 1861, when slavery was still legal in that state, she came to Iowa after the Civil War. She graduated in 1885, making her also the first female African American to graduate college in the state of Iowa.

The faculty of the 1887–1888 academic year sit for a photograph. From left to right are (first row, seated) Rev. C.N. Curtis, Ira Delong (principal of the preparatory academy), Minnie Edmand, Frederick Munz (German College), Pres. John McFarland, Ella Nicholson, Gus A. Walter, and C.M. Grumbling; (second row, standing) John Schalaganhauf (German College), Rev. W. Balcke (German College), Alexander Rommel (Conservatory of Music), and Lt. W.A. Dinwiddie, MD.

Members of the Hamline Society sit for a photograph in 1888. Pres. James Harlan advocated for the creation of the Hamline Society in 1855, the first literary society on campus. The society took its name from Bishop Leonidas Hamline, a popular speaker in Mount Pleasant at the time. Members competed in state oratorical debates.

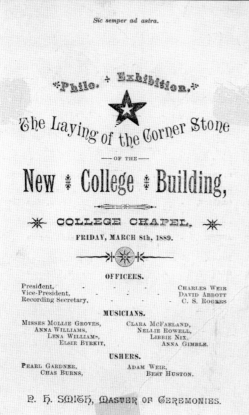

Sic semper ad astra.

Philo. ✦ Exhibition,✦

The Laying of the Corner Stone

— OF THE —

New ✦ College ✦ Building,

❋ COLLEGE CHAPEL. ❋

FRIDAY, MARCH 8th, 1889.

OFFICERS.

President, - - - - CHARLES WEIR
Vice-President, - - - DAVID ABBOTT
Recording Secretary, - - C. S. ROGERS

MUSICIANS.

MISSES MOLLIE GROVES,   CLARA McFARLAND,
ANNA WILLIAMS,   NELLIE ROWELL,
LENA WILLIAMS,   LIBBIE NIX.
ELSIE BYRKIT,   ANNA GIMBLE.

USHERS.

PEARL GARDNER,   ADAM WEIR,
CHAS BURNS,   BERT HUSTON.

P. H. SMITH, MASTER OF CEREMONIES.

Here is an invitation for the March 8, 1889, laying of the cornerstone for the building that would be the Chapel, billed as "the New College Building." The motto for the event, *sic semper ad astra*, is Latin for "thus always to the stars." Construction began in 1889, but was halted for funding reasons, hence the 1889 date chiseled on the building's foundation stone.

Two

BRICK LAYING
1890–1899

The last decade of the 19th century was an ambitious period in Iowa Wesleyan's history. President Charles Stafford's administration, which ran from 1891–1899, saw the addition of two major edifices on the campus grounds. The Chapel was completed in 1893, and Elizabeth Hershey Hall was finished in 1897.

The new buildings have interesting backstories. The construction of the Chapel began in 1889 but was halted due to a lack of funding. Therefore, the foundation stone reads 1889. However, the 1890s yielded more fruitful production, and the building was completed. The Chapel served for both religious services and scientific laboratory spaces. In 1899, James Harlan's funeral was conducted there.

Elizabeth Hershey of Muscatine was a committed member of the Methodist Church. She was a benefactor to many institutions, including an orphanage for the German Lutheran Society. In 1895, Hershey donated $10,000 to the university for a female dormitory. The building was realized just a few years later, complete with the latest improvements, including steam heating and electricity.

The 1897–1898 *Annual Register of the Iowa Wesleyan University* lists diverse courses and fields of study. A bachelor of arts program included study in Greek and Latin, as well as English, philosophy, and Bible studies. A bachelor of philosophy degree included coursework in German, French, Latin, and philosophy. A bachelor of science candidate took French, German, or Latin as well as mathematics, chemistry, oratory, and physics. A bachelor of letters student completed courses in mathematics, English, oratory, history, and Bible studies.

By the 1890s, student activities included the old literary societies, but also increasingly featured athletics. Football, basketball, tennis, and baseball were becoming more standardized by conference rules. Students utilized the gymnasium at the YMCA building in town, which was located where the post office is today.

Leisenrings Mt. Pleasant. IOWA.

Louisa Mason was the third African American student to graduate from Iowa Wesleyan, receiving her diploma in 1891. Her sister, Agnes Mason, graduated in 1887. Louisa was a member of the Ruthean Literary Society. She taught school in Missouri after graduating.

Snow is scattered on the grass in front of Pioneer Hall in this 1894 photograph. The building was half a century old at the time. Pioneer Hall holds the claim to be among the oldest academic buildings still in use west of the Mississippi River. Notice the wooden plank path in front of the building.

The Chapel was only two years old when this photograph was taken in 1895. Notice the tall spire on the east side of the building, as well as the young trees that have been planted in front. The path to the right is covered by wooden planks, but the path to the left toward Old Main is a dirt trail.

Rev. Charles Lewis Stafford (1871) guides a responsive reading at the Chapel around 1895. The Chapel auditorium served as a sanctuary for church services, while other rooms in the building provided spaces for scientific laboratories.

Professor William Mahaffie sits with his baby daughter in 1895. Mahaffie earned his bachelor's degree in science from Smithsonian College in 1875, and his PhD from Allegheny College in 1891. He served as the principal of the mechanical department and instructed courses in chemistry, physics, and biology.

The president's office, complete with a fireplace, was in the Chapel during the early years of the building. A portrait of Senator Harlan hangs on the wall.

Pres. Charles Lewis Stafford administered Iowa Wesleyan through the 1890s. His tenure proved to be one of the most significant in the school's history, and included the completion of the Chapel and Hershey Hall. Classroom and living spaces were expanded from the previous era, and with new spaces came more opportunities for students.

Marthine Dietrichson served as an instructor in vocal music during the 1890s. She studied for two years in Christiania, Norway, and four years in Rome, Italy, an example of Iowa Wesleyan's long tradition of international study and experience.

25

Old Main is shown here on a wintry day in about 1896. Less than 30 years before, seven Iowa Wesleyan students—Mary Allen Stafford (1869), Alice Bird Babb (1869), Hattie B. Briggs (1869), Alice Virginia Coffin (1869), Franc Rhodes Elliott (1869), Suela Pearson (1871), and Ella Stewart—met in the music room of this building and began the P.E.O. Sisterhood, which in time would become international in scope.

Construction workers have nearly completed Hershey Hall in this 1897 photograph. Elizabeth Hershey of Muscatine, an important local philanthropist who provided funds for several causes, had donated $10,000 for the building's construction.

A plank path runs in front of Old Main toward the Chapel in this 1897 image. Planks were an improvement over the previous dirt paths, and were in turn replaced by the cement paths used today.

Iowa Wesleyan's football tradition began in the late 1880s. Here, players from the 1897 team show early football gear. The pieces dangling around the necks of the standing players are nose guards.

The 1897 football team wore shirts with "IWU" stitched across the front. The 1897 season was an early success story for the university, with the team defeating Knox, Penn, Parsons, and Drake. Notice the ball in the lap of the player seated at center, which is more rounded than today's footballs.

Students lived in boarding homes before the construction of large dormitories. Here, students sit outside Mrs. E.M. Gray's house in 1899 on North Main Street. The construction of Hershey Hall began the transformation of student life, ushering in dormitory living.

The library was in Old Main before the turn of the 20th century. This image from 1899 shows a room in Old Main filled from floor to ceiling with books, as well as study tables for students and faculty.

Old Main hosted a museum with rare specimens from around the world. Note the elk on the left, the bison and bear at center, and the juvenile giraffe in the back. Iowa Wesleyan received a fantastic zoological collection in 1889 from Burlington taxidermist Chas Buettner, and the museum became an important learning resource in the 1890s.

This panoramic view from about 1899 shows the Chapel on the left and the German College on the right. The dirt road in the center is Main Street. This photograph is a good metaphor for the composition of Henry County and other portions of the Midwest during this period. The 1895 Census of Iowa counted 357 Henry County residents having been born in Germany and 469 having been born in Sweden.

Phi Delta Theta brothers play on a sand tennis court on campus west of the Chapel in 1899. Notice the long sleeves and long pants.

Students go for a picnic ride in about 1899. The Skunk River was a popular picnic place, and students also enjoyed walks along the rail line.

Students play tennis on a sand court on campus around 1899. The 1909 *Croaker* reports that Iowa Wesleyan tennis players competed against Parsons College and Simpson College.

Three

A NEW CENTURY
1900–1919

Iowa Wesleyan was nearly six decades old in 1900, a lifespan longer than the standard human life expectancy in the United States at that time. The curricula at the school were time-tested. The 1909 *Bulletin* reveals that students, depending on their course of study, took Greek, astronomy, literature, political science, education, history of philosophy, geology, Hebrew, and biology, as well as a host of other classes. All seniors took a course entitled Evidences of Christianity.

In the early years of the 20th century, Prof. Alexander Rommel's Conservatory of Music was nearly three decades old and well known. That German immigrant had made Iowa Wesleyan a music capital for the region. His work had received accolades from Eugene D' Albert in Berlin, whom many considered the greatest pianist in the world at that time. The conservatory provided oratorio performances, such as Handel's "Messiah," Haydn's "Creation," and Bennett's "Woman of Samaria."

The library facilities improved at the beginning of the century. The library moved from a single room in Old Main to larger spaces in the Chapel. One room was reserved for bookshelves, and a second room had a reference librarian and reading space. Students moved the books from Old Main to the Chapel with wheelbarrows.

The German College was active with its own curriculum and student body. The 1904–1905 catalog tabulates the coursework plan. Each year had three *termin* (semesters) instead of two. Courses included *lesen und rechtschreiben* (reading and correct writing), *weltgeschichte* (world history), *hoehere grammatik* (advanced grammar), and *kirchengeschichte* (church history). Students at the German College also took Greek, Latin, geology, and astronomy.

Student activity options were maturing. Students had the opportunity to join fraternities, sororities, and literary societies, as well as established athletic teams, including a men's basketball team, a women's basketball team, a football team, and a tennis team. Other organizations that were very active were the YMCA (Young Men's Christian Association) and the YWCA (Young Women's Christian Association). The 1909 YWCA program for Iowa Wesleyan members included discussions with the titles "Helping One Another," "God's Guiding Hand in Our Lives," and "Women of the Bible."

Female students attended the German College in the 19th century. This c. 1900 image shows, from left to right, students Carrie Eberspaecher, Carrie Mauch, and Oretta Bissinger. The German College offered different courses of study, including theology, classics, and science.

Mechanical Hall, shown here in about 1900, was erected to the east of Old Main in 1897 for the purpose of developing an engineering department. However, the program did not get underway, and the building signaled the end of the otherwise remarkable construction phase under President Stafford during the 1890s. Mechanical Hall is gone, but the bell seen here remains on the university green between Old Main and the Chapel.

During their *freizeit* (free time), female students in the German College hold a masquerade party around 1900.

Carrie Eberspaecher, photographed in 1901, studied music at the German College. She immigrated with her family from Stuttgart, Germany, in the 1880s.

Iowa Wesleyan's baseball team poses for a photograph in 1902. That year, the team started its first home game against Bradley Polytechnic College on a new baseball diamond, which the *Mt. Pleasant Journal* described as a field "in fine shape and no better or faster diamond can be made."

The first Iowa Wesleyan female basketball team is shown here in 1902. Sports at Iowa Wesleyan became more organized in 1888 with the development of a formal athletic association. A state athletic association was also formed in 1888, providing more opportunities in organized sports.

The library expanded from one room in Old Main to two rooms in the Chapel around 1903. Students moved the library collection from Old Main to the Chapel by rolling wheelbarrows filled with books across campus. A plank ramp helped the wheelbarrows enter the Chapel.

The ladies' basketball team is ready for the court in this photograph from the 1902–1903 season. The letters "I.W.U." are stitched on their arm sashes. The ladies' basketball team preceded the men's basketball team, which was not organized until 1908.

Students sit on the stairs of Hershey Hall in an image from about 1904. Around this time, the third floor of the hall was used as a women's gymnasium.

Students study in the Chapel library in 1904. The new library was a great improvement over the Old Main library, providing room for more books, study spaces, and reference assistance. Notice the card catalog to the left.

Notice the formal dress of the female students in this photograph from about 1904 at Hershey Hall. The matriarch of the dormitory was called the preceptress, and she ensured that the house rules were enforced.

This early view of the interior of the Chapel is from 1904 and predates the renovations of 1928 and 1929, which changed the stage area and the seating. The original seating, shown here, was in the style of church pews, indicating the primary function of the room. Senator Harlan's funeral was held here in 1899, with the room set in this fashion.

This view of Old Main and the Chapel may look familiar, but a closer look at the thin trees reveals that the image is much older, dating from about 1905.

This 1907 photograph looks north along Broadway Street, which was a dirt road at that time. The 1905 Census of Iowa shows that Iowa had 27,687 people aged 18 to 21 attending school, and almost half of them were female. About one in five Iowans in this age bracket were in school.

Julia McKibbin, preceptress of Hershey Hall, is seen in her parlor in 1908. McKibbin was a published author, and also served as a professor of history in the 1890s.

The 1909 football team sits for a photograph. The *Croaker* from that year stated, "Good, clean, spirited athletics are a valuable asset to a school and will do much to draw a desirable class of students to it."

Pioneer Hall in 1909 was almost 65 years old. In that year, students—depending on their academic track—took courses in Greek, Latin, mathematics, oratory, Biblical literature, German, biology, geology, economics, and astronomy, among others. All seniors took a course in Evidences of Christianity during their fall semester.

Prof. Friedrich Munz of the German College poses for a photograph in 1910. He himself graduated from the institution in 1887. Professor Munz served as president of the German College in the 1890s, and edited the German Methodist hymnals "Lobe den Herrn" ("Praise the Lord") and "Die Pilgerklange" ("Pilgrim Sound").

There is a carnival atmosphere at the square during homecoming festivities in about 1910. Notice the "W" stitched on the sweatshirts. The Brazelton Hotel is in the background with Jericho's Drugstore on the ground floor; that building is a renovated apartment space today.

The 1909–1910 Iowa Wesleyan basketball team poses for a picture. In the years before the 1921 Gymnasium, the basketball team would play in the YMCA building, which was located where the post office is today.

The 1909–1910 basketball team shows an early Iowa Wesleyan emblem, the "W." In 1909, the squad, in its second year of existence, won six out of ten games.

Dr. Lucy Booth served as a professor of history from 1897 to 1922. She received her bachelor's degree from Ohio Wesleyan in 1881 and her doctorate from Ohio State in 1892.

Students examine the science specimens in this image from about 1911. A few students playfully pose with a large wasp or hornet nest in the back center. A large cat specimen is on the right.

Athletics on campus were in full swing in the 1910s. Here, a giant football—marked with the year 1913—sits behind the squad. The 1913 *Croaker* shows a campus enthused with school spirit, including long banners strung between trees that read "Beat Parsons."

The Blazer's Club poses for a picture in about 1919. With a wink and a nod, redheads on campus formed their own organization in 1918. The group had no particular goals or objectives other than meeting to have fun.

Four

A ROARING, ELECTRIC AGE
1920–1929

Many consider the 1920s to be a watershed decade in US history. It is the decade when automobiles officially replaced horses, electric lights went from luxury to necessity, and people tuned into favorite programs on the radio. Ideas that had existed as possibilities on paper for decades suddenly became goods that could be purchased at a local store. The Roaring Twenties were in full swing.

The 1920s were roaring at Iowa Wesleyan as well. Two new buildings, built facing each other, reveal the dual role of secondary education in the 20th century: academics and athletics. The P.E.O. Sisterhood successfully financed the first dedicated library building in the school's history, an edifice for academics. Across the way, the new Gymnasium gave Iowa Wesleyan students a state-of-the-art pool and basketball court, an edifice for athletics.

The *Annual Catalog of Iowa Wesleyan College* for the 1924–1925 academic year shows a new precision to the course load. Instead of following a course of study that was "scientific" or "philosophical," majors were now more technical and specified, the result of newly accrued knowledge bases. For example, students could pursue a degree in agriculture, as opposed to a more general science route. Courses in agriculture during the 1924–1925 school year included corn production, animal feeding, animal husbandry, horticulture, poultry husbandry, soils, and farm accounting.

A popular professor during this era was Prof. Harry Jaques in the biology department. Courses in his department included botany, bacteriology, plant pathology, tree study, entomology, and genetics. Meanwhile, education students in the 1920s took courses in the history of education in the United States, childhood and adolescent development, methods of teaching, and rural school management. Iowa Wesleyan graduates received a state certificate to teach if they had successfully completed six semester hours in psychology and fourteen semester hours in education.

While many argue that baseball, basketball, and football have altered over the decades due to changes in players' sizes and gear, track meets—featuring athletes running around a circuit—have largely stayed the same since the time of the ancient Greeks. In 1923, an Iowa Wesleyan runner, Russell Prewitt, bested the competition at Penn with a 4:42 mile time, still a respectable time today.

Hershey Hall students pose for a photograph in 1920. Student organizations, including team sports, sometimes included neckerchief accessories. The 1925–1926 Hershey Hall house regulations stipulated quiet study hours for each day.

An alumni banquet is held in the dining area of Hershey Hall in 1920. The hanging electric lights were an increasingly common feature in buildings during this era, as the innovations of the 19th century were now becoming accessible by the 1920s.

Thomas Myers had the honor of plunging the first spade into the soil during the ground-breaking ceremony for the new Gymnasium in 1921. Dr. Myers was the oldest living alumnus in 1921. He served in the 1st Iowa Volunteer Cavalry during the Civil War.

The basketball team shows some smiles in this 1921 photograph. During the 1920 season, the team finished with a record of eight wins and four losses, including a 66-13 win against the Fairfield Legion.

The new Gymnasium in 1921 was one of the great athletic complexes in the region. It provided Iowa Wesleyan with its own swimming pool and basketball court. Mount Pleasant in the 1920s had two large indoor sporting complexes: Iowa Wesleyan's Gymnasium and the YMCA building. Notice the dirt road.

Everett Reed began work at Iowa Wesleyan as a maintenance custodian in 1922, ultimately becoming maintenance head during his many years of service. Over the decades, Reed's profession saw modernizing advances in lights, plumbing, and building codes.

In 1923, funding was provided for a new annex section to Hershey Hall, which is visible at left center. Notice the coupe on the street. The 1920s were the decade that saw the official replacement of the horse and wagon with automobiles, the rise of radio, and the proliferation of electricity.

The old football field, located in the field that would later become the site of Sheaffer-Trieschmann Hall, is shown here in 1923. Behind the team are wooden bleachers. Old Main and Pioneer Hall are in the background. Protective face masks were still 30 years in the future.

This image shows the basketball court in the Gymnasium in about 1925. While this space is no longer a basketball court, the area is still used for athletic training. Notice the 1920s net at top center.

A track team member stands in racing gear in about 1925. Notice that his shoes are cleats. By the 1920s, the sports gear industry had developed into a large enough enterprise for specialized equipment.

Students pose around 1925 in the Gymnasium pool. The first row is dressed in the full-body swimsuits fashionable in the 1920s, but the second row is dressed in gowns and tunics.

These students are putting the "roaring" into the Roaring Twenties at this pool party in about 1925. Balloons hang in the background. A diver jumps off the board. Balls are floating in the pool. It was the era of jazz and flappers.

Swimmers work on their diving skills in this 1927 photograph in the Gymnasium pool. Swimming had become a common recreational activity by the 1920s, and the full-body swimsuit was proper attire.

Crews dig out the foundation of the future P.E.O. Memorial Library. The P.E.O. Sisterhood agreed to build a memorial library at Iowa Wesleyan, the location of the organization's founding. The new Gymnasium is visible at far right, and the German College building is visible on the left.

Mary Allen Stafford, one of the original founders of the P.E.O. Sisterhood, stands second to the right in the first row during the P.E.O. Memorial Library's cornerstone laying ceremony in 1927. She was married to Charles Stafford, who had served as president of Iowa Wesleyan from 1891 to 1899. Charles and Mary Allen together were integral to the addition of three iconic campus buildings: the Chapel, Hershey Hall, and the P.E.O. Memorial Library.

Vina Bowden was the chairwoman of the building committee for the P.E.O. Memorial Library. Here, she lays mortar with a trowel on a cornerstone in 1927. The P.E.O. Sisterhood approved the construction of the library at Iowa Wesleyan at a convention in Minneapolis, Minnesota.

Alice Scott, the president of the Supreme Chapter of P.E.O. in 1927, stands at the left. Ola Miller, the first vice president of the Supreme Chapter, stands next to her. In addition to the short hairstyles and hats, the vehicles in the background help to date the image to the 1920s.

The first vice president of the Supreme Chapter of P.E.O., Ola Miller, stands on the stairs of the P.E.O. Memorial Library at the cornerstone laying ceremony in 1927. She stated, "May this building long serve to enrich and ennoble the lives of countless youths as they come and go throughout the years."

The P.E.O. Memorial Library is pictured behind snow-covered trees. The P.E.O. Sisterhood had donated $100,000 for the construction of this library, which served as both a memorial to the organization's founders and as a resource for the students of Iowa Wesleyan.

The 1928–1929 Chapel remodel removed the tall tower spires. However, the east tower remained taller than the west tower for the next 30 years.

These ladies are dressed in football attire on a homecoming float that reads "Pickin' on the Peacock," a reference to the Upper Iowa Peacock. In 1929, possibly the year of this photograph, the Tigers were the undefeated Iowa Conference champions, and they did "pick on the Peacock," beating Upper Iowa 26-0. The German College is in the background.

Five

DEPRESSION AND WAR YEARS
1930–1949

They were the best of times; they were the worst of times. The long-term reality of the Great Depression took a few years to settle in during the early 1930s. Conditions soured, then seemed to improve, then soured again. Iowa Wesleyan's Gymnasium become even more important after a fire consumed the YMCA building in town in 1932, destroying local high school and athletic facilities that had served Mount Pleasant since the 19th century.

Iowa Wesleyan made major scientific contributions during the Depression. Dr. Thomas Poulter (1923), who headed the division of physical sciences, mathematics, and astronomy, sent a letter to Rear Admiral Richard Byrd, the famous South Pole explorer. The admiral was impressed with Dr. Poulter's scientific research questions and invited him to the 1933 expedition to Antarctica. Concurrently, one student in the physics department at Iowa Wesleyan was James Van Allen (1935), who would also make his own scientific discoveries after graduating.

The football team had six straight winning seasons from 1928 through 1933.

The war years from 1941 to 1945 brought an irony to campus demographics. On the one hand, college-aged men were called into service abroad. On the other hand, Iowa Wesleyan became a posting for the US Army Air Force, which brought men to Mount Pleasant. Iowa Wesleyan faculty provided courses for the servicemen on English, mathematics, history, physical education, and other topics. Government buildings popped up on campus, including a large wooden barracks for the servicemen. This barracks, called Broadcourt, continued to operate as a dormitory following the war.

The years immediately following the war saw the emergence of new American popular culture. In 1949, Iowa Wesleyan's first student union building was established in one of the wooden government barracks built during the war. This first student union building was adjacent to the Gymnasium. The student union featured tables for bridge and other card games. Refreshments like coffee, tea, and ice cream were available. Students could also play ping-pong and other games.

This 1931 image shows the removal of the rear portion of the Harlan-Lincoln House. This part of the house was the older section of the structure, from before the Harlans expanded the home in the 1870s.

The sisters of Beta Pi Theta in 1931 were language scholars. Beta Pi Theta is a national French-language organization, and the 1931 *Croaker* noted, "Their monthly meetings are made interesting by the study of art and music as well as the study of French literature."

The 1931 brothers and sisters of Beta Beta Beta were engaged in biological study. Etelka Rochenbach (second from right) and Don Hookum (far right) presented at the Iowa Academy of Science meeting.

"Heave! Ho!" Students play "pushball" in 1931, a back-and-forth contest involving a giant ball. The long-term reality of the Depression was sinking in, but students still enjoyed goofing around.

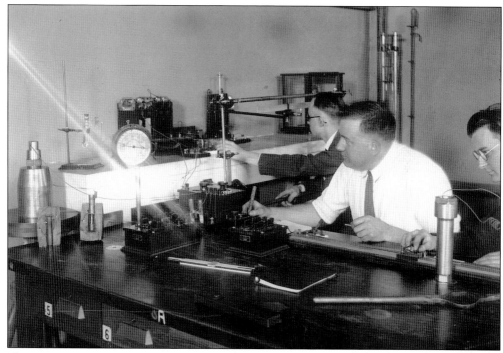

This is a rare glimpse inside the physics laboratory in the old German College in the 1930s. Dr. Thomas Poulter (center) ventured with the explorer Richard Byrd to Antarctica, where he was credited with saving the admiral's life from carbon monoxide poisoning.

Army barracks are under construction near Hershey Hall in this 1943 image. The drop in male enrollment was offset by the arrival of a military unit, the 82nd Detachment of the US Army Air Force.

Iowa Wesleyan played a role in the war effort. In 1943, the university became a site for an Army Air Forces college training program. Government barracks, shown here, were built to provide for the training of servicemen. These barracks would remain after the war as Broadcourt dorm.

Prof. Harry E. Jaques taught biology at Iowa Wesleyan from 1912 to 1947. He directed the Iowa Insect Survey and also served as president of the Iowa Academy of Science.

The Harlan Hotel on Jefferson Street was used as a women's dormitory at the time of this 1943 photograph, as the servicemen were residing in Hershey Hall. James Harlan lived in this building in the mid-19th century.

Army air servicemen were housed in Hershey Hall in 1943 and 1944. The college was able to serve students as well as the national war effort during the war, providing facilities, courses, instructors, and training for servicemen.

This 1940s view of the chemistry laboratory inside the Chapel shows the instruments the students were using for scientific experimentation. The Chapel remained an important facility for laboratory space, as did the old German College, until the completion of the Trieschmann Hall of Science in 1961.

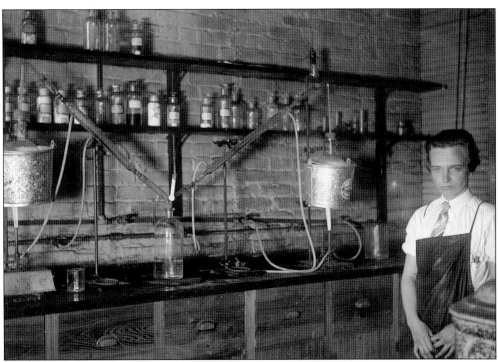

Laboratory work in the Chapel during the 1940s was in the pre-plastic age. Notice the glass containers on the shelf. The 1946 *Croaker* explained that the exact location of the chemistry department is not necessary to note, because "one has only to enter the Chapel door and be confronted with the odor of that well known compound, hydrogen sulfide, and he knows the exact location."

Frank D. Throop Memorial Hall was built in 1947 adjacent to the Chapel, which is seen at left. The building contained the alumni office, classrooms, and the freshman chemistry laboratory.

Jump ball! The Tigerettes, in dark uniforms, compete at the 1947 Amateur Athletic Union (AAU) national tournament in St. Joseph, Missouri. That season, the team had several wins by large margins, defeating Keosauqua 65-28, Burl Gremlins 53-22, and What Cheer 49-23.

The Tigerettes receive a trophy at the 1947 National Women's Basketball Tournament held in St. Joseph, Missouri. They defeated the Jayhawkers of Pittsburg, Kansas.

It is study time in the P.E.O. Memorial Library in 1948. In that year, Iowa Wesleyan had 20 academic departments in four divisions. The Division of the Natural Sciences included a Department of Mathematics, Mechanical Drawing and Astronomy.

The original student union building from 1949—with the white siding and "Student Union" sign near the entrance—was refashioned from one of the Army barracks built on campus during World War II. The Gymnasium is to the left of the student union.

Broadcourt—the dormitory refashioned from the old Army barracks—remained in use until 1952. The 1948–1949 *Annual Catalog* offered courses as diverse as Art of the American Indian, Scientific German, Radio Script Writing, and Economic Entomology.

This 1949 photograph was taken in the first student union building. The young men are all in ties. A live band plays in the background.

Six

HIGH TIMES
1950–1959

Iowa Wesleyan had one of its most substantial growth periods during the 1950s. The postwar years resulted in an entirely new campus environment. Due to the GI Bill, expanding vocational outlooks, and a growing economy, college education was increasingly viewed as a means to career advancement.

Broadcourt, a former government barracks, remained from the war years as the men's dormitory. In 1950, enrollment had grown to over 800 students, with 290 of them being veterans. Academic curricula were updated, including a return of foreign language requirements and a modernization of the education department's program. The music department joined the Southeast Iowa Symphony Orchestra in 1956.

Old Main turned 100 in 1955, and those 19th-century brick buildings that dominated the campus landscape were now complemented by a new architectural style from the 20th century. Pres. J. Raymond Chadwick outlined an ambitious campus building and expansion program. A new dormitory, Sheaffer-Trieschmann Hall, multiplied student capacity, and the new Holland Student Union provided additional venues for student socializing. The Harlan-Lincoln House was restored and turned into a museum in 1959. The old German College, used in the 1950s as a physics building, was covered with ivy and showed its age.

Students had more academic options in the 1950s than in any other period, a reflection of the expanding economic opportunities in the postwar world. Students could pursue a traditional humanities or natural sciences track, as well as social sciences like sociology, economics, or business administration. Students could also study athletics and physical education, revealing the cultural force that these fields had become by the 1950s.

The 1950s ushered in the postwar American culture, all flowering on campus. Rock-and-roll music came into full swing. Students danced at the campus hop at the student union and congregated at soda fountains that served Coca-Cola. Iowa Wesleyan's Tigers and Tigerettes left their mark on the regional athletic landscape in the 1950s. The football team posted winning seasons in seven out of the ten years of that decade. The ladies' basketball team produced All-American athletes who competed on the national stage under the leadership of coach Olan Ruble.

J. Raymond Chadwick served as president of Iowa Wesleyan from 1950 to 1961. His tenure resulted in one of the most ambitious periods in the university's life, including the construction of Sheaffer-Trieschmann Hall, the Holland Student Union, and, in the year of his death in 1961, Trieschmann Hall of Science.

Students in the P.E.O. Memorial Library find books in this image from about 1950. The Doric columns exemplify the classical Greek style of the building. Students in the foreground are talking with library staff, and students in the background are busy working on assignments.

Female students dine by candlelight in Hershey Hall around 1950. Dining facilities were moved to the new Holland Student Union building in 1957.

Plates and silverware are set in the dining room in Hershey Hall in this image from about 1950. Ice cream was scooped into bowls on the serving table to the right.

The old German College was well-covered in ivy in this photograph from about 1950. The building served as the German College from its construction in 1873 until 1909, at which point it became a physics building. Laboratories were also stationed here.

From left to right sit center Cliff Brees, coach Lawrence "Pops" Harrison, coach Everett Jarvis, and guard Dick Furjanic, who led the 1952 Tigers to a record of 7-1. The team had one of the best defensive lines that year, giving up only 25 points the whole season.

74

The 1952 football team was one game short of a perfect season. The season included several blowout wins, including a 34-0 win over Central, a 58-0 win over Eureka, and a 62-0 win over Culver-Stockton.

Coach Olan Ruble talks with Iowa Wesleyan All-Americans Dorothy Welp (left) and Janet Thompson during the 1952–1953 year. In 1953, these two student-athletes played for Team USA at the first women's world championship, which was held in Santiago, Chile. Team USA won the championship.

The guys relax with a game of billiards in about 1953. This game room was in the original 1949 student union building. The wooden planks forming the wall are evidence of the structure's previous life as an Army barracks. A box with a Sunkist Oranges label is on the back shelf.

The 1953 Tigers football team won the Iowa Conference championship, prevailing over Wartburg 33-14. The undefeated Tigers went on to compete at the Corn Bowl against Western Illinois, their only loss that year.

Students enjoy the soda bar in the original student union building around 1954. Glass bottles of Coca-Cola syrup can be seen on the shelf at bottom center.

Light refreshments are served at the original student union building around 1954. Coca-Cola bottles and Nesbitt's orange soda are stocked on the shelves. The student to the right enjoys a Drumstick ice-cream cone.

Students socialize in the original student union building around 1954. On the back wall, there is a poster for 7 Up. Chocolate sundae fudge is also behind the counter. The original student union building lasted from 1949 to 1957, when it was replaced by the Holland Student Union.

This aerial view was photographed around 1954. There is no Holland Student Union building yet. The German College, used at this time as a physics building, is seen in the large open field at center, near the future location of Trieschmann Hall of Science. Throop Hall, which is no longer standing today, can be seen peeking out of the trees to the right of the Chapel, across the street from the German College.

Visitors and alumni enjoy dinner in the basement of Hershey Hall in 1955 during Homecoming Week.

Students are hard at work inside the P.E.O. Memorial Library in about 1955. While it appears to be all serious, notice the fancy reindeer-themed Christmas sweater on the scholar at left. The 1955 *Croaker* shows another young man wearing a ski-themed Christmas sweater, photographic proof that the Christmas sweater tradition goes back to at least the 1950s.

Students relax in Sheaffer-Trieschmann Hall in about 1956. In addition to leisure reading and discussion, a Women's Recreation Association of Iowa Wesleyan was organized in the academic year 1958–1959, providing activities like bowling, ping-pong, swimming, volleyball, and other social opportunities for female students.

Sheaffer-Trieschmann Hall is shown here in 1956, just a few years after it was finished. In these early years of the female dormitory, a student council supervised the living standards of the residence.

Students look at a map of Greece during the 1956 Campus Bible Conference. Iowa Wesleyan hosted these annual conferences that featured lectures related to biblical scholarship. Lectures were presented by faculty as well as United Methodist clergy.

Students are gathered in the Chapel in 1956. During the 1955–1956 year, the college-civic theater held several plays, including the comedic yet insightful coming-of-age show *Bernadine*, as well as the play *Twelfth Night* by William Shakespeare.

Students bundle up for the cold cross-campus walk in this image from about 1955. The 1955–1956 annual bulletin noted that a full semester's tuition cost $190. A student could rent a typewriter for a semester for $6, although business students had access to typewriters without any additional costs.

Up and over! Mike Fenn vaulted 11 feet, 8.25 inches in this track meet against Simpson in 1956.

The Business and Economics Club is ready for the working world in this 1957 image. Coat and tie were standard wear in this era, even for college students. The 1954–1955 *Iowa Wesleyan College Annual Catalog* lists courses in economic geography, principles of economics, business law, principles of insurance, statistics, and others.

The finishing touches are being placed on the new John Wesley Holland Student Union in 1957. The grass has not yet been replanted. The Holland Student Union building features classic mid-20th-century architecture, utilizing large window panels framed in aluminum, allowing the outside to penetrate inside, a very different style than the 19th-century brick buildings.

Students decorate the Christmas tree during the Holland Student Union's first holiday season in 1957. A new and popular holiday tune from that year was Bobby Helms's "Jingle Bell Rock."

Students play ping-pong in the Holland Student Union during the building's first year in 1957. The building has served the multiple roles of gathering space, cafeteria, meeting area, and office space for decades.

Science advisors meet in the P.E.O. Memorial Library around 1957 to discuss the spaces, equipment, and curriculum necessary for a modern science hall. Dr. James Van Allen (1935) is standing at the head of the table. Women were on this committee that planned the building that would be Trieschmann Hall of Science. Martha Crane Caris and Meta Jane Masters Brooks are seated on the left.

Cheerleaders pose for a photograph in 1957. That year's *Croaker* commented that there is "an American idea that participation in organized physical activity is a part of our way of life. . . . Competitive play, for participants and spectators, is a symbol of a free way of life, of a necessary give and take, of a sense of sportsmanship."

Students nock arrows during an archery activity in 1957. Iowa Wesleyan has long emphasized the importance of gaining new experiences and trying new activities.

Iowa Wesleyan All-American Barbara Sipes (center) watches as a basket is made during the 1957 AAU National Tournament in St. Joseph, Missouri. Sipes received one of the first athletic scholarships to Iowa Wesleyan, and was named into the AAU National Hall of Fame in 1963.

Students select music at a jukebox at the Holland Student Union in 1958. Some chart toppers that year were "Rockin' Robin" by Bobby Day and "Yakety Yak" by the Coasters.

Coach Ruble speaks with Barbara Sipes (left) and Sandra Fiete. Sipes was selected for the All-American team in 1955, 1957, and 1958, and she led Team USA to the world championship game in Rio de Janeiro, Brazil, in 1957, beating the Soviet Union. Fiete was selected for the All-American team in 1957. These two student-athletes toured Russia in 1958 with Team USA.

Workers clean the north face of the Chapel during the 1959 renovation. Throop Hall, the building with white siding, has since been replaced by a brick addition.

Workmen remodel the east tower of the Chapel to level it with the west tower during a renovation in the 1950s. Ivy was also removed from the walls, and the building's exterior took its present shape.

Seven

THE BOOMER ERA
1960–1979

The Baby Boomer era invigorated the college campus environment with modernized facilities and social activism. The 1960s was the most recent era of large-scale additions to the campus, resulting in three new buildings. The Trieschmann Hall of Science was dedicated in 1961, George B. McKibbin Hall housed its first students in 1966, and the J. Raymond Chadwick Library was constructed in 1968, though that building was not formally named until 1972. Thus, the 1960s are one of the decades of great transformation in the history of the university.

Social activism was a component of 1960s campus culture, and that is observed in the listings of required courses. The 1969–1970 catalog lists American Identity in World Perspective; Totalitarianism and the Free Society; Communications, Culture, and Society; and Responsible Social Involvement among the list of required courses.

Student life improved during this period with the new library. The three-floor facility provided the books, journals, audio-visual equipment, microfilm, and study space necessary for the increasing flow of information in the late 20th century, as well as the resources needed for a wider palette of sources and perspectives incorporated into the curricula. A three-story mosaic of a one-celled Paramecium, spanning the main stairwell, was designed by Stan Wiederspan in the art department.

The 1960s and 1970s were important periods in Iowa Wesleyan basketball history. The Tigerettes received national attention in 1962. Coach Ruble's basketball team had produced champions and All-Americans, and in 1962, the Tigerettes received even wider national attention when they played against the Soviet women's team at Cottrell Gym in Mount Pleasant. The Soviet basketball tour involved not only the AAU, Iowa Wesleyan, and Coach Ruble, but also parties from the US State Department and the Soviet Union. The Russian players and Soviet government officials overnighted in Sheaffer-Trieschmann Hall. The Russians prevailed, but the game was a contest and an experience for the ages.

The men's basketball team was a conference force from 1969–1974, holding a conference record of 54 wins and only 6 losses over those years. The Tigers won the conference title each of those six years. In 1969, coach Dean Davenport was named Coach of the Year in the Prairie Conference. Thus, the 1960s and 1970s were a golden age for Iowa Wesleyan basketball.

Students are busy at work in their Hershey Hall dorm room in 1960. Notice the portable radio on the desk.

This 1960 image of the Chapel during wintertime shows an exterior that is the same as today. The tall spires are gone. The chemistry laboratory, which had been in the basement of the Chapel since the 1890s, was soon to be relocated to the future Trieschmann Hall of Science. The Chapel increasingly became a center for local arts and cultural programs, like the Southeast Iowa Symphony Orchestra.

Female students are moving into their dorm rooms at Sheaffer-Trieschmann Hall in about 1960.

Federal loans provided the funds to expand Sheaffer-Trieschmann Hall in 1960. Here, workmen build additional wings onto the rear of the building.

The 1960 addition to Sheaffer-Trieschmann Hall doubled the capacity for female students living on campus. Men resided in Hershey Hall at this time, which originally had been a female dormitory.

Students work in the laboratory in Old Main in 1960. The 1959–1960 *Iowa Wesleyan College Bulletin* listed courses in tree identification, ecology, general botany, ornithology, entomology, and comparative vertebrate anatomy, among others.

The Tigers pile up against an opposing team at McMillan Park in 1960. While the 1960–1961 team only won a single game that year—defeating Simpson College 26-0—they still had the experience and life-long memories of playing college football.

The 1959–1960 basketball team finished the season with seven wins and fifteen losses. However, the team achieved a four-game winning streak, and lost multiple games by only a few points, including an 81-80 loss against Dubuque University. Before the end of the decade, the Tigers would be champions.

This architectural drawing of the Adam Trieschmann Hall of Science became a reality in 1961. Dr. James Van Allen (1935) led a team of Iowa Wesleyan alumni scientists to advise President Chadwick on the facilities and needs of science education, modernizing the learning experience.

"C.C.C.P." is embossed on the sweatshirts of the men's and women's Soviet national basketball teams. The Russians played Iowa Wesleyan at Cottrell Gym in November 1962. Some 1,300 tickets were sold for the competition.

Dr. R. William Poulter (center) leads a biology class in the new Trieschmann Science Hall in about 1962. This new space was a major upgrade in science equipment and facilities compared to the facilities available in the Chapel basement. Note the rows of new microscopes.

Dr. Martin Allwood, professor of sociology, assists with registration in about 1965. Dr. Allwood conducted summer programs in Sweden and the Soviet Union, a coordinated project with the Anglo-American Center in Sweden.

A snack bar, shown here in 1965, once served refreshments on the first floor of the Holland Student Union. Adjacent to the snack bar was a game room.

Beanie caps are handed out to freshmen in about 1965. Freshmen on many college campuses during the mid-20th century donned such caps, which identified their first-year status.

The deans meet. From left to right, James Stefl (men's counselor), Joseph Mauck (student personnel services), and Carol Nemitz (women's counselor) examine a document in about 1965. Dean Nemitz served the institution for decades, and many alumni noted her positive influence on their lives.

George B. McKibbin Hall was built as a residence hall for men in 1966. The original bidding invitation to contractors called for a three-story, 47,000-square-foot building with the intention of housing 200 students.

The new male dormitory, McKibbin Hall, relieved the pressure on Hershey Hall to house male students. The functional, mid-20th-century architecture matches the female dormitory, Sheaffer-Trieschmann, constructed the decade before. Both male and female students now had state-of-the-art living quarters.

The interior of McKibbin Hall featured lounge spaces that encouraged social interaction. The new dormitories were a physical manifestation of the explosive college enrollment rates during the post-war era. Iowa Wesleyan had 829 students in the academic year 1969–1970, the highest enrollment in its history as of the writing of this book in 2022.

This aerial view of campus was captured in 1966 or 1967. Toward right center is the Holland Student Union, constructed in 1957, and at top center stands Trieschmann Hall of Science, built in 1961. McKibbin Hall, at bottom center, was built in 1966. However, the absence of Chadwick Library determines that this image was taken before 1968.

Within Throop Hall, once beside the Chapel but no longer standing, Prof. Paul Ernsberger facilitates a language lab in 1968. At that time, Iowa Wesleyan's language department included instruction in French, Spanish, and German.

Dr. Martin Allwood sits in the second row, fifth from the right, with students from Iowa Wesleyan and other institutions at a 1968 summer session at the Anglo-American Center in Sweden. The program allowed students from Iowa Wesleyan to have cross-cultural exchanges with students from Sweden and the Soviet Union.

A French class meets outside on the grass on a nice day in 1968. The P.E.O. Memorial Library is visible in the background. Iowa Wesleyan has always prided itself on the low student-to-instructor ratio, giving students close access to the faculty, allowing for memorable and effective learning experiences.

Students are seen working in the Hershey Hall lounge in 1968. Some of the courses included in the 1968–1969 catalog were creative photography, playwriting, field biology, and analytical chemistry.

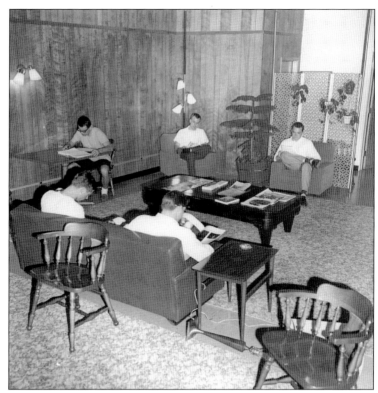

In 1969, one hundred years after Arabella Mansfield's bar examination, Prof. Louis Haselmayer, pictured here, confirmed that Mansfield was not only the first female attorney in Iowa, but also the first female attorney in the United States, an achievement recognized that year by the National Association of Women Lawyers. Professor Haselmayer served as president from 1970 to 1982.

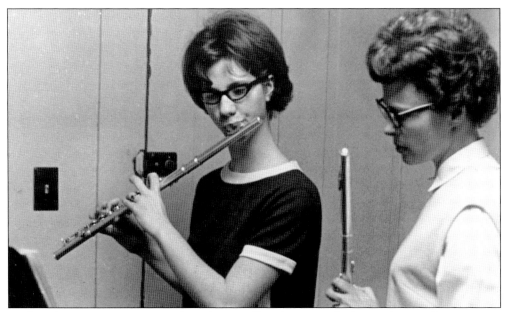

Prof. Ruth Keraus instructs a student during a flute lesson in the late 1960s. Professor Keraus started teaching at Iowa Wesleyan in 1960, and her career spanned the remainder of the century. She also conducted the Southeast Iowa Symphony Orchestra.

Iowa Wesleyan (light uniforms) goes for a score against St. Ambrose about 1970. From 1969 through 1974, the men's basketball team held the league title, a golden era of basketball at the university.

The new library is built and in use, but there is no lettering above the front entrance. This image was taken between 1968 and 1971, because the building had not yet been formally named after J. Raymond Chadwick.

A worker places the letters spelling "J. Raymond Chadwick Library" above the library threshold in 1972. The building was named to honor the memory of the late past president who transformed the campus environment.

President Haselmayer officiates the dedication of the new library in May 1973. Ruth Chadwick, the widow of Dr. Chadwick, is to the right. Chairman E.A. Hayes looks down at a dog that is trying to steal the show.

Students get their lunch buffet style at the Holland Student Union in 1973. A student guide booklet from the 1971–1972 academic year states, "Each year a food popularity poll is taken to determine the student preference in each area of meal planning. . . . To satisfy the student with the heavy appetite, seconds are offered on all items except steak on Saturday night."

Dr. George LaMore mentors a student in about 1975. Dr. LaMore was a popular and sought-after instructor in religion and philosophy, and he led workshops during Iowa Wesleyan's annual Campus Bible Conferences.

This aerial image shows the campus around 1975, when there was a tennis court between Old Main and the Chadwick Library.

Pres. Louis Haselmayer works away at the typewriter in the university archives around 1976. Dr. Haselmayer produced several works on Iowa Wesleyan University, writing on the university's history and noted alumni.

A student is hard at work in McKibbin Hall in 1977. A radio is on the desk, and the sports page is tacked onto the wall.

Prof. Connie Gartin (left) helps students in 1979. Professor Gartin brought to campus the nursing experience she gained from working in the Mental Health Institute in Mount Pleasant, playing an instrumental role in the creation of the nursing program in the 1970s.

Prof. Jerry Naylor paints a theater prop in 1979. During the 1979–1980 year, Iowa Wesleyan students performed Shakespeare's *Richard III*.

Bikes line this 1979 photograph of the entrance to Sheaffer-Trieschmann Hall. Also visible are the Greek affiliations in the windows, including Alphi Xi Delta and Pi Beta Phi.

Students hit the books in this photograph from the Chadwick Library in 1979. Psychology classes in 1979 included educational psychology, abnormal psychology, computer applications in the social sciences, and experimental psychology.

Eight

THE COMPUTER AGE
1980–PRESENT

Iowa Wesleyan's history spans from pioneers to personal computers, and the story continues to the present day. The computer age brought new electronic tools and resources to students' fingertips, and knowledge is more accessible in the current age than ever before. Yet many of the goals of the present institution remain in common with the original goals established at its founding in 1842. Iowa Wesleyan, today as then, centers around developing enlightened, well-rounded students who can make the world, in degrees both big and small, better.

Iowa Wesleyan's tradition of scholarship and progress enters its 180th year in 2022. The school has a rich history of diversity reaching back to its pioneer founders and continuing to the present. Susan Mosely Grandison graduated in 1885, the first African American college graduate in the state of Iowa, and that tradition of diversity continues. Iowa Wesleyan today is the most diverse university environment in Iowa. The university also treasures the high number of international students hailing from Asia, Australia, Africa, Europe, Central America, South America, and Oceania. Iowa Wesleyan has also cultivated a tradition of educating large numbers of first-generation college students.

Iowa Wesleyan's story has come full circle. In the pioneer age, Arabella Babb Mansfield (1866) broadened the horizon of possibilities for women, and in the computer age, astronaut Peggy Whitson (1981) blasted through Earth's atmosphere, reaching new heights not only for women but for all humankind. Dr. Whitson served as the first female commander of the International Space Station during an expedition in 2007–2008. By 2017, Dr. Whitson had spent 665 days in space, the most for an American woman. She has told Iowa Wesleyan students, "Don't put limits on your dreams or yourself."

Dr. Whitson shows Iowa Wesleyan students that the sky is not the limit. Rather, the sky is just the beginning. Imagine what stories might be told at the university's 250th anniversary in 2092.

Brass instructor Lon Harding (center) practices with his students in about 1980. Harding headed the Iowa Wesleyan Jazz Ensemble, as well as the wind ensemble group, performing concerts at the Chapel Auditorium.

Students research newspaper archives on microfilm reels around 1980. While electronic archival systems have become commonplace in the 21st century, microfilm is often still retained as a durable, long-lasting backup for irreplaceable materials.

A student reads the newspaper in the Chadwick Library in about 1980. A challenge of the post–Baby Boomer era in higher education locally and nationally was stagnated enrollment due to gaps between generations. However, college enrollment improved again.

The Black Awareness Board (BAB) held a fashion show in the Chapel in 1984. The BAB was incorporated in 1972, and its purpose was to illustrate the long heritage of African Americans on and off campus, sponsoring lectures, concerts, and events.

The Science Club displays the fruits of their labor in about 1984, the different sizes of birdhouses providing homes to different species of local birds. Professor Roland Shook is at far left.

Prof. Dolores Poulter "D.P." Wilson (1963) instructs a class in the Chadwick Library around 1985. Professor Wilson was in her third decade teaching at Iowa Wesleyan at this time.

Prof. L. Joel Brown provides piano instruction in about 1985. Professor Brown performed recitals for the university and the community, including works by Bach, Schumann, Chopin, and Mozart.

Professor of English Mildred Bensmiller assists a student in the English writing lab around 1985. Iowa Wesleyan today serves many first-generation college students, and special emphasis is given to writing help and mentorship.

The Tigers celebrate a victory during the 1986–1987 season. In that year, the men's basketball team had its first winning season in 12 years, finishing the regular season with a record of 16 wins and 10 losses.

Repairs are underway after a January 1989 fire at Old Main. The fire damaged the third floor, destroying the roof and the cupola, as well as musical equipment. Fortunately, many of the historical P.E.O. Sisterhood possessions housed there were undamaged. President Prins committed the institution to rebuilding the iconic building in 1989 and 1990.

A newly built cupola is ready to be set on the roof of Old Main in 1990. The 1989 fire had destroyed the original cupola, so great attention was made to build a new cupola that matched the original due to the structure's historical significance.

On April 14, 1990, a helicopter lifted the new cupola over the campus and set it on the restored Old Main building. In 1854, Old Main sustained damage from storms while still under construction, and in 1990, it came back from a fire. Old Main is a survivor.

Iowa Wesleyan offers a picturesque college experience featuring a green central common. Some of the eastern white pine and tulip trees on campus have witnessed several generations of students pass between the buildings.

Prof. Chip Charleston shows students in 1991 how an electroencephalograph (EEG) machine works to measure brain activity. The advent of such electronic monitoring systems provides nurses and doctors with more detailed and accurate biometric data.

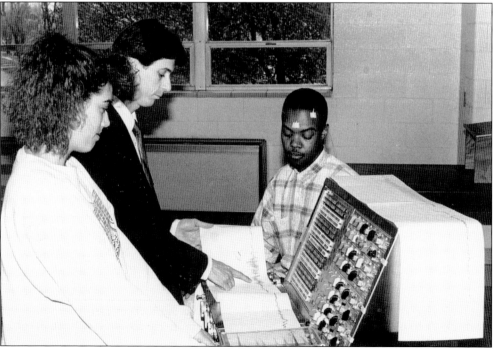

Iowa Wesleyan has a long tradition of welcoming international students. In this 1991 photograph, Steven Eau Claire instructs an English language class for students from Japan and other nations.

The Lady Tigers are about to record a hit as the runner approaches first base during the 1990–1991 season. The following year, the softball team finished with a solid record of 14 wins and 10 losses.

Librarian Pamela Ross shows a student how to search the ProQuest electronic database in 1992. In this image are examples of two eras of information management: the card catalog in the background and the new computer data retrieval system in the foreground.

Prof. William Weiershauser assists a student with his literature study in the library in 1992. The *Iowa Wesleyan College Bulletin* from that era noted, "The ownership of a dictionary is required in freshman English." English classes in 1992 included Shakespeare, the Psalms, and modern poetry.

Prof. Vince Mahoney (right) instructs students with educational software in 1992. His background in science and math education resulted in the utilization of computers and electronics in the classroom.

Prof. Ann Klingensmith (center) works with art students during a printing operation in 1992. Professor Klingensmith's work has been exhibited in numerous venues, including at Columbia College in Missouri and in the magazine *American Artist*.

The first organized soccer club at Iowa Wesleyan was formed in 1992. The students who formed the club were largely international students, including several men from Japan, as well as others from Canada, Kenya, and Nepal.

Pres. Robert Prins presides over Founders Day in 1992 in the Chapel. Founders Day is celebrated on February 17, commemorating the day in 1842 when the Iowa Territorial Legislature passed a bill to establish a literary institute in Mount Pleasant.

Prof. D.P. Wilson (1963) has been teaching biology at Iowa Wesleyan since the 1960s. Here she helps student Wayland Rucker with a microscope in 1995.

Prof. Robert Bensmiller guides communications students through the electronic matrix of computers, video screens, and sound equipment in 1995. The skills that these students are learning would empower them for the 21st century.

Students crunch away at their keyboards in the computer lab in the Trieschmann Hall of Science in 1995. The computer age was taking shape. "Files" and "folders" increasingly referred to data stored on hard drives, not paper products.

The Howe Student Activity Center is under construction in the year 2000. The building was dedicated in 2001, named after lifelong supporters Stanley and Helen Howe of Muscatine. The 35,000-square-foot building provided modernized athletic and conference facilities, preparing Iowa Wesleyan for a new century.

Many of the images in this book were archived and preserved for years by Joy Conwell. Until her last days in 2021, she worked to preserve the memory of Iowa Wesleyan University.

Dr. Peggy Whitson (1981, left) and Dr. D.P. Wilson (1963, right) have both made lasting impressions on the university. Dr. Whitson, a student of Dr. Wilson's while she attended Iowa Wesleyan, went on to become a NASA astronaut, logging hundreds of days in space.

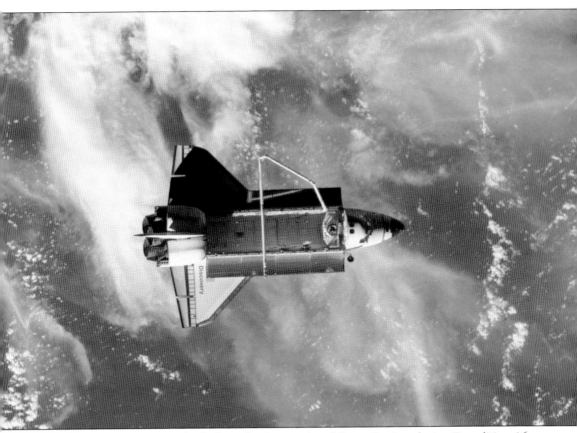

Space Shuttle *Discovery* undocks from the International Space Station during Expedition 16 in 2007. Expedition 16 was commanded by Dr. Peggy Whitson, the first time an American woman had served as commander of the ISS. (Courtesy of NASA.)

DISCOVER THOUSANDS OF LOCAL HISTORY BOOKS
FEATURING MILLIONS OF VINTAGE IMAGES

Arcadia Publishing, the leading local history publisher in the United States, is committed to making history accessible and meaningful through publishing books that celebrate and preserve the heritage of America's people and places.

Find more books like this at
www.arcadiapublishing.com

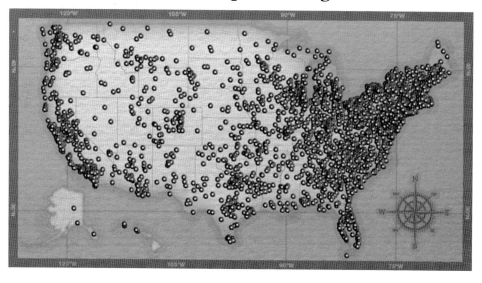

Search for your hometown history, your old stomping grounds, and even your favorite sports team.

Consistent with our mission to preserve history on a local level, this book was printed in South Carolina on American-made paper and manufactured entirely in the United States. Products carrying the accredited Forest Stewardship Council (FSC) label are printed on 100 percent FSC-certified paper.

MADE IN THE USA